More or less?

Addition and subtraction

All rights reserved. This book is sold subject to the condition that it shall not, by way of trade or otherwise, be lent, hired out or otherwise circulated without the publisher's prior consent in any form of binding or cover other than that in which it is published and without a similar condition, including this condition, being imposed upon the subsequent purchaser.

No part of this publication may be reproduced, stored in a retrieval system, or transmitted, in any form or by any means, electronic, mechanical, photocopying, recording or otherwise, without the prior permission of the publisher. This book remains copyright, although permission is granted to copy those pages labelled PHOTOCOPIABLE for classroom distribution and use only in the school which has purchased the book, or by the teacher who has purchased this book, and in accordance with the CLA licensing agreement. Photocopying permission is given for purchasers only and not for borrowers of books from any lending service.

British Library Cataloguing-in-Publication Data
A catalogue record for this book is available from the British Library.

ISBN 0-590-53582-X

Published by Scholastic Ltd
Villiers House
Clarendon Avenue
Leamington Spa
Warwickshire CV32 5PR

© 1996 Scholastic Ltd
123456789 6789012345

AUTHOR
Shirley Beswick

SERIES CONSULTANT
Sheila Ebbutt
Director of BEAM (Be A Mathematician) which is supported by Islington Council

CURRICULUM LINKS
Ian Gardner, Maths Curriculum Adviser, (England and Wales), Julie Parkin, with Edinburgh Centre for Mathematics Education (Scotland) and Michael Wallace (Northern Ireland)

The publishers wish to thank the following individuals and organisations for their invaluable help in developing the *Maths Focus* concept: Jayne de Courcy, Courcy Consultants; Dr Daphne Kerslake; West Sussex Maths Centre, West Sussex Institute; Oxfordshire Maths Centre; Edinburgh Centre for Mathematics Education; David Bell, Assistant Director for Education, Newcastle-upon-Tyne; Professor Geoffrey and Dr Julia Matthews

EDITORIAL TEAM
Angela Dewsbury and Jo Saxelby-Jennings

SERIES DESIGNER
Joy White

DESIGNERS
Louise Belcher

COVER PHOTOGRAPH
© Scholastic Inc.

ILLUSTRATORS
Val Biro, Roma Bishop (John Martin & Artists), Sonia Canals, Debbie Clark (Simon Girling Assoc.), Trevor Dunton, Emma Holt (Sylvie Poggio), Claire James (Graham-Cameron), Lorna Kent, Derek Matthews, Chris Russell, Peter Read, Mick Reid (Peters, Fraser and Dunlop) and The Drawing Room.

POSTERMAT
Emma Holt (Sylvie Poggio)

Designed using Aldus Pagemaker
Processed by PAGES Bureau, Leamington Spa
Printed in Great Britain by Ebenezer Baylis & Son, Worcester and George Over, Rugby

© Material from the National Curriculum, Scottish 5–14 Guidelines and the Northern Ireland Curriculum is Crown copyright and is reproduced by permission of the Controller of HMSO, 1995.

CONTENTS

4	*MATHS FOCUS* OFFERS...
6	HERE'S THE MATHS
8	CURRICULUM LINKS
9	USING AND APPLYING GRID

DIAGNOSTIC ASSESSMENT
10	PICKING APPLES

ASSESSMENT DOUBLE-CHECK
14	MAKING NUMBERS

REINFORCEMENT ACTIVITIES
16	LADYBIRD SPOTS
18	MAGIC BOX
20	GUESS HOW MANY
22	FISH AND THE WORMS
24	NUMBER PICTURES
26	SNAKE GAME
28	COUNTING SHEEP
30	TOWERS

ENRICHMENT ACTIVITIES
32	COLOURED FISH
34	APPLE PAIRS
36	NUMBER SHAPES
38	WHAT'S THE DIFFERENCE?
40	CALCULATOR ADDING
42	SECRET NUMBERS

RESOURCES
44	PICKING APPLES
45	APPLE PAIRS
46	0–11 NUMBER CARDS
47	12–20 NUMBER AND OPERATION CARDS
48	PHOTOCOPIABLE OF POSTERMAT

MATHS FOCUS

Maths Focus can be used to:

- ▶ assess children's knowledge and skills;
- ▶ offer reinforcement activities to develop understanding;
- ▶ provide enrichment activities to consolidate and extend the learning;
- ▶ develop skills and ability in using and applying mathematics.

DIFFERENTIATION

1 *Maths Focus* offers structured progression of content and skills through the Kits 1–5* and provides links with all UK national curricula. With a particular clakss or year group, you may use activities from more than one kit to cater for all ability levels. Each book focuses on a specific mathematical concept, with activities set in a range of contexts – including games, stories, problems, everyday situations and puzzles – so that children learn to use their mathematics flexibly and appropriately.

2 Assessment activities allow you to evaluate the children's ability to use and apply the mathematics they have learned.

3 Understanding is developed through two types of activity:
▶ **Reinforcement activities** – which increase children's confidence by concentrating on specific concept or skill and presenting the maths in a variety of contexts;
▶ **Enrichment activities** – which consolidate and extend children's learning in more open-ended contexts.

4 Extension ideas at the end of each activity offer ways for more able children to go further in their exploration of a concept.

*See inside back cover for overview of kits and curriculum coverage.

offers...

Maths Focus can be used in a variety of ways to support your teaching of mathematics and your style of teaching, allowing you to use the activities with individuals, groups or the whole class.

FLEXIBLE RESOURCE

Use **Maths Focus** activities alongside a published scheme to:
- develop children's understanding of specific concepts in a greater range of contexts;
- assess children's understanding of a concept, and then to support or extend it with differentiated activities;
- focus on the using and applying aspect of the mathematics curriculum.

If you don't use a published scheme use **Maths Focus**:
- as a core resource when planning your own scheme of work;
- to teach and assess specific concepts.

USING & APPLYING

Aspects of **Using and Applying** covered by each activity are given in the teacher's notes. To help with your planning, the grid on page 9 and the teachers' notes highlight how problem solving, communication and logical reasoning are built into each activity.

USING TALK

All teachers' notes pages offer questions you can ask children to encourage them to talk about what they are doing. Use the questions while they are working to focus their mathematical thinking or at the end of the activity to assess their level of understanding. Most pages also offer:
- **Here's the maths** – explanations of the maths included in the activity;
- **What to look for** – diagnostic pointers to help you to assess whether the child has achieved the mathematical aim of the activity;
- **More help needed** – ways to help children are who struggling with the activity.

ASSESSMENT

Maths Focus offers two types of assessment to be used when you feel appropriate to plan the best way forward for each child.

- You may want to use the **Diagnostic assessment** activity at the start of teaching a concept to establish the existing level of understanding. Alternatively, use it after some initial teaching, to provide a check on progress.

- The **Assessment double-check** allows you to assess the child's understanding of the concept as a whole, to see how their learning has progressed.

RANGE OF RESOURCES

Maths Focus kits come with a full-colour laminated postermat for each book. This flexible wipe-clean resource can be used with a number of the activities in its book and also as a general mathematics resource. Each book has a black and white photocopiable version of its postermat, to use with the activities and for permanent recording of the children's work. Extra postermats are available separately (see inside back cover).

The activities in each book are planned to use a range of mathematical resources, including counting apparatus, number lines and grids and calculators. Mental maths is emphasised throughout.

Activities in this book have an emphasis on addition. However, these activities must go hand in hand with work on subtraction if the children are to gain a full understanding of either operation.

Here's the maths...

Addition and subtraction

What's involved – addition

- Children learning addition need to develop a thorough understanding of the process involved, and an ability to use effective methods of computation. To achieve this they need many opportunities to use practical, mental and formal addition in a variety of everyday situations and cross-curricular activities.
- When children make patterns with a group of objects, for example, five counters, they will explore and notice things about putting the counters into smaller groups. It is from here that the idea of addition will develop. The reverse of this process is to start with two separate groups of objects and combine them to make one group. Children need experience of both of these types of addition. When they first encounter it, children will see splitting up a group of 5 counters into 2 and 3 as very different from combining 3 counters and 2 counters to make 5. It is only after experience that they will realise that these can be treated as the same operation.
- Children need plenty of experience of using and handling small numbers of objects in a variety of ways, such as sorting, grouping, splitting up sets of numbers and counting. This will help them to add sets of objects with confidence. Through handling objects

LANGUAGE OF ADDITION

- While gaining understanding of addition through various practical activities, children need also to experience situations which involve discussions such as:
How many are there altogether?
How many have we got between us?
How many were there to start with?
Can you give yourself 5 more than I've got?
- They need to be introduced to the mathematical language appropriate to using:
  • objects to model real situations;
  • number lines - counting 'forwards' and 'backwards';
  • calculators - *What is the calculator doing to each of these numbers? How are the numbers changing?*

- It is important that the children use precise mathematical language as soon as possible to avoid confusion later on. For example, if they learn to say 2 + 3 = 5 as 'two and three *makes* five' and 5 - 3 = 2 as 'five take away *leaves* two' they are using two different ways to read the '=' sign. It is best, therefore, to use 'equals' as the way to read this sign to avoid confusion.

USE OF SYMBOLS

▸ Children need lots of practical experience and discussion to learn the basic idea of operations with numbers, and to build up a mental idea of them. The use of the arithmetical symbols should come at the end of this stage, alongside the use of apparatus.
The symbols may confuse children if introduced too soon.

Subtraction

the children will develop an understanding of the process of addition – that adding two numbers results in a bigger number.

▸ Through handling objects, using number lines and calculators, and talking about what they are doing the children will begin to gain a mental understanding of addition. This is vital and will help them to develop skills of estimation and checking their answers.

▸ When the children are involved with the practical adding of two sets of objects they should also be encouraged to compare the two sets – which has most/fewest.

▸ Most problems involving addition can also be solved by subtraction, since addition and subtraction are inverse operations. While the emphasis in this book is on addition some of the activities will also involve subtraction since these two operations go hand in hand. While developing an understanding of addition and subtraction by solving problems children should also have opportunities to gain a practical understanding of the relationship between the two operations.

BUILDING ON KNOWLEDGE OF ADDITION FACTS

▸ Ultimately, addition is a tool for solving mathematical and 'real-life' problems. Only when children have an understanding of the process should we begin to help them to develop skills at recalling addition facts efficiently and quickly.

KEY FACTS

▸ There are five aspects of addition which the activities in this book cover.

These are:
▸ addition of two sets;
▸ knowledge and understanding of addition;
▸ counting on using a number line;
▸ introduction of the addition sign;
▸ building on a knowledge of addition facts.

KEY WORDS

more, less
all together
equals
fewest, most
forwards
backwards
add
take away
difference

MORE OR LESS?
MATHS FOCUS – NUMBER KIT 1

7

Curriculum links

This chart outlines the particular strands and statements from each of the UK curriculum documents for maths that apply to the content of this book.

The processes outlined opposite show how this maths is applied to a range of contexts and how outcomes are reported.

MATHEMATICS IN THE NATIONAL CURRICULUM (ENGLAND AND WALES)

This book covers the following statements from the Key Stage 1 Programme of Study for Number:
◗ Children should be given opportunities to:
• develop flexible methods of working with number, orally and mentally;
• use a variety of practical resources and contexts;
• use calculators as a means to explore number;
• record in a variety of ways, including ways that relate to their mental work.
(1a, c, d [part] and e)

Pupils should be taught to:
◗ Understanding relationships between numbers and developing methods of computation
• explore and record patterns in addition and subtraction;
• know addition and subtraction facts to 20. (3b [part] and c [part])
◗ Solving numerical problems
• understand the operations of addition, subtraction as taking away and comparison, and the relationship between them;
• begin to check in different ways..., and gain a feel for the appropriate size of an answer. (4a [part] and d)

MATHEMATICS 5–14 (SCOTTISH GUIDELINES)

This book covers the following strands of the Attainment Target Number, Money and Measurement:
◗ Add and subtract
• **Add and subtract:** mentally for numbers 0 to 10, in applications in number, measurement and money, including payments and giving change to 10p (Level A).
◗ Patterns and sequences
• **Work with patterns and sequences:** simple number sequences (Level A);
• **Work with patterns and sequences:** whole number sequences within 100 (eg 10, 15, 20..., or 89, 79, 69... .)(Level B).

NORTHERN IRELAND CURRICULUM FOR MATHEMATICS

This book covers the following strands of Number from the Programme of Study at Key Stage 1:
◗ Patterns, relationships and sequences in number
Pupils should have opportunities to:
(b)   explore and record addition and subtraction patterns.
◗ Operations and their application
Pupils should have opportunities to:
(a)   understand the operations of addition and subtraction (as take away or comparison or complementary), add and subtract initially using small numbers, use these skills to solve number problems involving whole numbers;
(c)   know addition and subtraction facts initially to 10, and then to 20.
◗ Pupils should use calculators to explore, through play and number games, how a calculator works and how it can be used as a tool for calculating with realistic data.

8 MORE OR LESS?
MATHS FOCUS – NUMBER KIT 1

Using and applying

All of the activities in **Maths Focus** involve applying mathematics. This chart will help you to identify which strands of Using and Applying Mathematics are part of each activity. Problem-solving and Enquiry (Scottish 5–14 Guidelines) and Processes (NI Curriculum) are also addressed through these statements.

Activities	Problem Solving	Communication	Logical Reasoning
DIAGNOSTIC ASSESSMENT			
Picking apples	Work independently. Work systematically. Check that s/he has given all the possible results. Select the appropriate maths.	Record appropriately. Talk about the work. Explain the results.	Show understanding of number bonds. Show understanding of the addition of two sets – both practically and mentally.
ASSESSMENT DOUBLE-CHECK			
Making numbers	Know how to tackle the problem. Work systematically. Check results. Complete the task.	Record (maybe with conventional symbols). Explain what is involved in the task	Show an understanding of how to 'make' a number by adding or taking two other numbers.
REINFORCEMENT ACTIVITIES			
Ladybird spots	Work independently. Use addition to find the answer.	Talk about what is involved using maths language such as: add, makes, equals, same as, more, less.	Understand pictorial and numerical recording. Notice patterns in addition.
Magic box	Use 'magic box' appropriately. Work collaboratively and independently.	Explain what he or she is doing. Record answers.	Understand when an answer is unreasonable.
Guess how many	Choose appropriate objects. Guess, then check.	Record systematically. Discuss the work.	Make reasonable guesses which are getting closer each time. Understand that the smaller the object the bigger the number.
Fish and the worms	Work systematically. Work independently. Select the appropriate mathematics.	Record appropriately. Discuss the work.	Notice and explain the pattern. Show an understanding of the subtractions.
Number pictures	Work systematically. Work as an individual within their pair.	Talk about the game.	Work out which two numbers are needed for a certain space. Make his or her own number picture.
Snake game	Work as an individual within the pair. Work systematically.	Record appropriately. Talk about the game.	Realise that the higher dice number the further forward they will go, and ivce versa.
Counting sheep	Match each object in the book to the correct number. Work methodically.	Discuss what is involved.	Work out answers to the questions. Device own method of recording.
Towers	Work collaboratively. Devise own method of recording.	Discuss work. Record appropriately.	Work out the difference.
ENRICHMENT ACTIVITIES			
Coloured fish	Use the key. Work systematically.	Talk about the work. Talk about how quickly he or she can work out the answers.	Spot that they can work out some answers at the same time, such as 3 + 1 and 1 + 3.
Apple pairs	Use a strategy to work out where the cards are. Work collaboratively.	Explain what she or he is doing and how he or she is working them out.	Notice that some number bonds give the same answer.
Number shapes	Devise a way for solving the problem. Work systematically. Work independently.	Record appropriately. Discuss the work.	'Count on' when adding. Find that for some shapes the same number can be used in each corner to make the middle one.
What's the difference?	Work systematically. Work collaboratively and individually.	Explain work and recording.	Work out the difference. Show an ability to check answers – maybe with cubes.
Calculator adding	Use the constant function in order to solve the problem. Work systematically.	Explain work. Record findings.	Make good guesses. Make understandable errors (if any).
Secret numbers	Work independently.	Talk about the difference between addition and subtraction	Work out that adding a number makes you move forward; and subtracting makes you move backwards.

MORE OR LESS?
MATHS FOCUS – NUMBER KIT 1

TALK ABOUT

▶ 'How many apples in each of these two baskets?'
▶ 'Have you found all the ways of filling the baskets? How do you know?'
▶ 'How is this pair of baskets different from this pair?'
▶ 'Can you think of a way to check that you have found all the different ways without using the apples?'

DIAGNOSTIC ASSESSMENT

Picking apples

Key aims

▶ To discover how confident a child is about:
• counting to 10;
• using number bonds to 10;
• combining two sets of objects;
• recording number bonds and addition answers.

What you need

▶ at least 1 activity sheet 'Picking apples 1' and 1 activity sheet 'Picking apples 2' per child
▶ 1 'Picking apples' resource sheet per child (see page 44)
▶ scissors
▶ pencils, coloured crayons or pens

Organisation

▶ Write a different number, between 3 and 10, on each activity sheet 1 so that the children can be assessed individually while working in a group.
▶ Have extra copies of activity sheet 1 ready, particularly for those children who start with a small number or who require many more baskets into which to sort their apples.

The activities

▶ Give each child a 'Picking apples 1' activity sheet and a copy of the resource sheet. Explain what to do:
• cut out the number of apples written in the small apple on the activity sheet and put them on the apple tree;
• 'pick' the apples from the tree, put them into the two baskets and record on their activity sheet how many apples in each basket;
• put the apples back on the tree and 'pick' them again, this time putting a different number of apples into each basket.
▶ Leave them to complete the activity, finding as many 'combinations' they can, continuing on the back if necessary.
▶ If a child completes this activity sheet without difficulty give her 'Picking apples 2'.
▶ Explain that this time the apples have been picked and put into two baskets each time. In each case the children must find out how many apples there are altogether and write the number in the small apple at the side.

Where next?

▶ If a child completes both activity sheets easily, you will need to try an assessment at a higher level.

MORE OR LESS?
MATHS FOCUS – NUMBER KIT 1

Name

Picking apples 1

Your number of apples is:

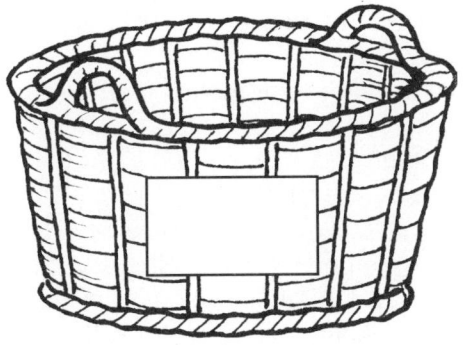 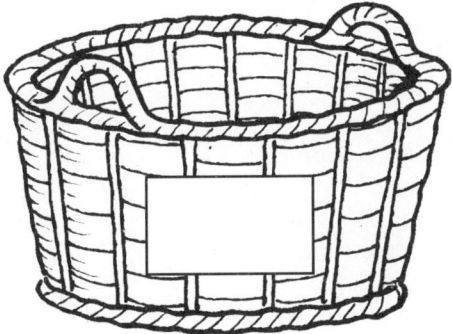

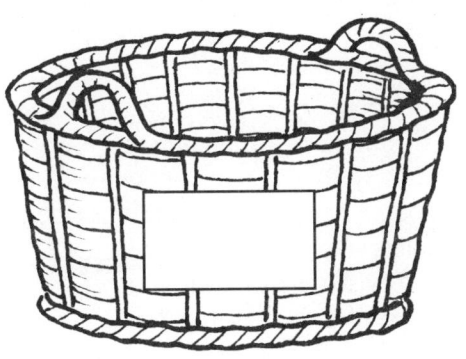 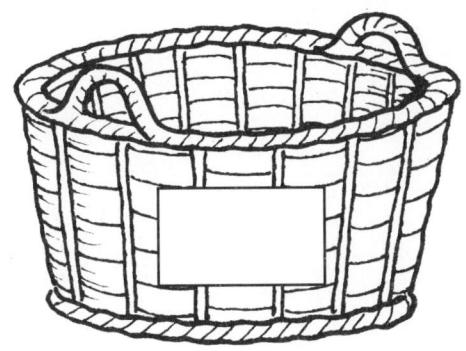

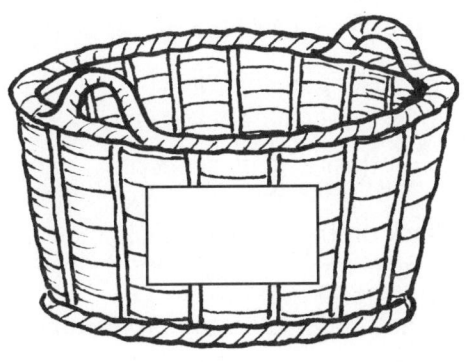 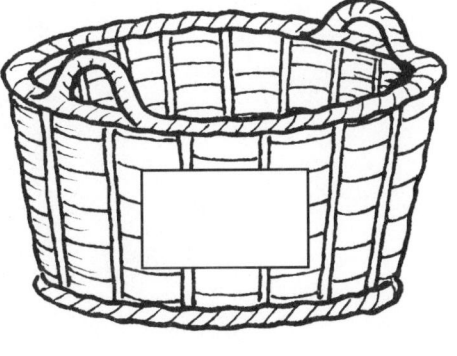

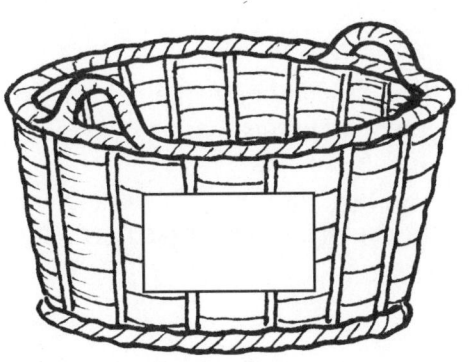 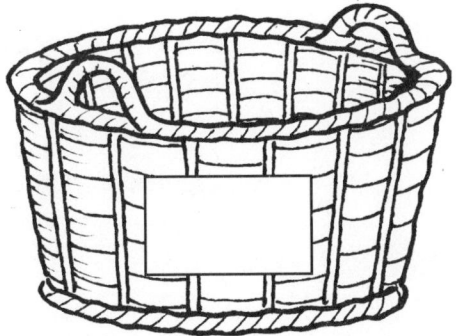

ASSESSING USING & APPLYING

PROBLEM SOLVING
▶ Does the child:
• work independently?
• work systematically?
• check that she or he has given all the possible results?
• select the appropriate maths?

COMMUNICATION
▶ Can the child:
• record appropriately?
• talk about the work?
• explain the results?

LOGICAL REASONING
▶ Does the child:
• show understanding of number bonds?
• show understanding of the addition of two sets – both practically and mentally?

DIAGNOSTIC ASSESSMENT

Assessing understanding

▶ Look for the following to indicate that the children are ready for **Enrichment activities**. They may:
• show a good understanding of number bonds and not need to use the apples. For example, they may give you another number bond for the two baskets without using the apples;
• record appropriately and be able to explain their recording;
• work systematically through the two sheets, and be able to explain what they did;
• show that they are able to use mental methods to work out the answers;
• give themselves appropriate 'apple sums' for the second sheet and work out the answers.

▶ Some children may be able to check they have all possibilities for 'Picking apples 1' by writing two columns of numbers starting with the total number of apples at the top of the first column, working down to zero, and with zero at the top of the second column working up to their number.

▶ Look for the following to indicate that the children are in need of further work on these concepts of addition and subtraction. They may:
• lack confidence in working out the tasks, asking questions or for reassurance from you or others in the group;
• work in a random way through the activity sheet 'Picking apples 1', and be unable to give all the number bonds for their number of apples;
• be unsure about how to record their work;
• have difficulty in explaining their methods;
• have difficulty counting.

Children who need more help

▶ If any children are lacking in confidence, or are having more difficulty than you anticipated, you may want to work with them on the first activity, 'Picking apples 1', doing the recording for them while they tell you how many apples to put in the baskets each time.

▶ You could give them some small cubes or counters to use when working on the second sheet.

▶ Children who do not understand the problem need to return to activities which involve practical adding and finding number bonds, such as the **Reinforcement activities** 'Ladybird spots' (page 16) and 'Fish and the worms' (page 23).

▶ Children who show difficulty in mental addition could go on to **Reinforcement activities** 'Magic box' (page 18) and 'Snake game' (page 26).

▶ Children who need help with practical addition could go to **Reinforcement activity** 'Number pictures' (page 24).

Picking apples 2

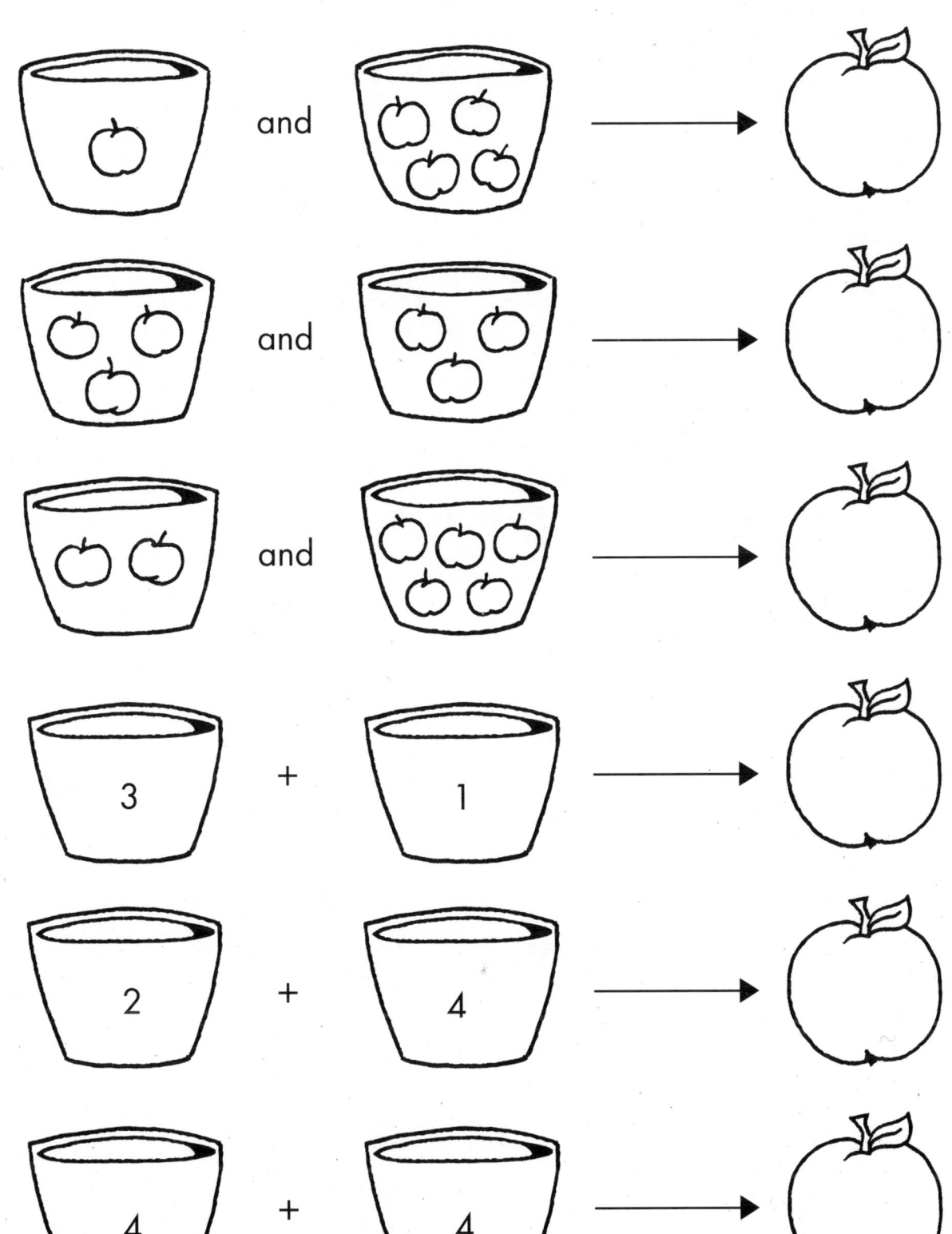

Try and do some more 'apples sums' on the back.

ASSESSING USING & APPLYING

PROBLEM SOLVING
◗ Does the child:
• know how to tackle the problem?
• work systematically?
• check results?
• complete the task?
COMMUNICATION
◗ Does the child know how to record (maybe with conventional symbols)?
◗ Can the child explain what is involved in the task?
LOGICAL REASONING
◗ Does the child show an understanding of how to 'make' a number by adding or taking two other numbers?

TALK ABOUT

◗ 'Can you think of any more ways?'
◗ 'How can you check you've made your number?'
◗ 'How do you know you haven't used that way already?'
◗ 'Which way was easy/difficult to find? Why?'

ASSESSMENT DOUBLE-CHECK

Making numbers

Key aims
◗ To assess if a child appreciates:
• how numbers can be made from two other numbers using addition or subtraction;
• that there are many ways of 'making' a number using addition and subtraction;
• how to record addition and subtraction tasks.

What you need
◗ 1 activity sheet per child
◗ cubes or small objects
◗ pencils
◗ 1 set of 1–20 number cards per child (see pages 46–47)
◗ 1 set of various +, –, = sign cards per child (see pages 46–47)

Organisation
◗ Write a different number on each child's activity sheet so that they can be assessed individually. Start with numbers between 5 and 10 but use higher numbers with those children who will find these easy. Have counting objects available for children who wish to use them.

The activity
◗ Give out the activity sheets and explain to the children that they are to use the objects, number and sign cards to think of as many ways possible to make their number, and record these on the sheet.
◗ Set out an example using two number cards and the '+' card.
◗ Leave them to complete their sheet. You may want them to continue with another number on the back of their sheet.

Assessing understanding
◗ Look for:
• confidence in finding many different ways, including addition and subtraction of more than two numbers;
• an ability to check their answers, using cubes or calculators, for example.

Where next?
◗ If the children still lack confidence, they will need further **Reinforcement activities** before they move on to tasks set in less visual or practical contexts, or using larger numbers.
◗ You can use this **Assessment double-check** activity at any time, using different numbers, to see how the child's understanding has progressed.

Name _____

Making numbers

My number is: ☐

I can make it like this:

PHOTOCOPIABLE

MORE OR LESS?
MATHS FOCUS – NUMBER KIT 1

15

REINFORCEMENT ACTIVITY

Ladybird spots

Key aims
▸ To introduce or reinforce patterns of addition.
▸ To carry out and record practical additions.

What you need
▸ at least 1 activity sheet per child
▸ pens, pencils

The activity
▸ Together look at the activity sheet. Talk about how ladybirds have spots on their backs.
▸ On a spare copy of the sheet, draw three spots on one side of a ladybird and two spots on the other. Ask the children how many spots there are on each side and write in the numbers in the boxes. Now ask them how many spots there are on the ladybird altogether. Show them where to write this number.
▸ Explain that they are going to imagine they have seen a ladybird and draw in the spots it has. They then record the number of spots on each side and the number in total on their activity sheet.
▸ Tell them to make sure that all of their ladybirds are different. When they are clear on what to do leave them to complete the sheet.
▸ Have more sheets available for children to create many different ladybirds.

Extension ideas
▸ Draw on the spots yourself with numbers above 10, for which the children can write number statements.
▸ Write in the number statements on the sheet for the child to draw on the spots.
▸ Write in the number of spots on the ladybirds as numerals, so the children don't have the spots there to count.

USING & APPLYING

PROBLEM SOLVING
▸ Work independently.
▸ Use addition to find the answer.
COMMUNICATION
▸ Talk about what is involved using mathematical language such as: add, makes, equals, same as, more, less.
LOGICAL REASONING
▸ Understand pictorial and numerical recording.
▸ Notice patterns in addition.

TALK ABOUT
▸ 'How many spots on this side? How many on the other side?'
▸ 'How many altogether?'
▸ 'Does it matter which side we start counting from?'
▸ 'Do any of your ladybirds have the same number of spots altogether?'

HERE'S THE MATHS
▸ Children use their knowledge of number patterns to split the numbers into two.
▸ Looking at the ladybird with 3 + 1 spots and the one with 1 + 3 spots and noticing that they both have the same total number of spots introduces the idea of commutativity – that the order of the numbers in an addition sum does not matter.

WHAT TO LOOK FOR
▸ Does the child notice patterns of addition?
▸ Can the child make a pictorial and numerical recording?

MORE HELP NEEDED
▸ Children who count inconsistently need practice counting objects.
▸ Children who find it difficult to split numbers into groups need to do this with real objects.

16 MORE OR LESS?
MATHS FOCUS – NUMBER KIT 1

Name _____

Ladybird spots

How many spots?

☐ and ☐ → ☐

☐ and ☐ → ☐

☐ and ☐ → ☐

☐ and ☐ → ☐

PHOTOCOPIABLE

MORE OR LESS?
MATHS FOCUS – NUMBER KIT 1

REINFORCEMENT ACTIVITY

Magic box

Key aim
◗ To help to develop a mental understanding of both addition and subtraction.

What you need
◗ 1 decorated box
◗ marbles
◗ 1 activity sheet per child
◗ pencils

Organisation
◗ Make a 'magic' box to use with this activity – a shoe box will do. Cut out a small hole at the top of the box and have a door at the bottom of the box to let the marbles out.

The activity
◗ Put the box in the middle of the group and put in, for example, five marbles. Then put in, for example, two more. Ask the children how many are in the box altogether.
◗ Open the magic door to let the marbles out and let the children count them to see if they said the right number.
◗ Repeat with different numbers of marbles, sometimes adding more, sometimes taking them out.
◗ Let each child have a turn at being the 'Magic box assistant', deciding how many marbles to put in or take out for the rest of the group to say how many in total.
◗ Give out the activity sheets and explain that the number on the box is the number of marbles already in and that the numbers by the arrows show how many more marbles they are putting in or taking out, depending on the direction of the arrow.
◗ Ensure they understand what to do and leave them to complete the sheet.

Extension ideas
◗ Starting with a given number of marbles, explore the number patterns which occur when you add/take away a set number of the marbles to/from the box each time (repeated addition/subtraction).
◗ Explore the number pattern which occurs through following a specific rule of adding so many marbles then taking away so many, repeating this sequence each time.

USING & APPLYING

PROBLEM SOLVING
◗ Use the 'magic box' appropriately.
◗ Work collaboratively and independently.

COMMUNICATION
◗ Explain what she or he is doing.
◗ Record answers.

LOGICAL REASONING
◗ Understand when an answer is unreasonable.

TALK ABOUT
◗ 'How close was your guess?'
◗ 'How did you work it out?'
◗ 'How can you check you have got it right?'

HERE'S THE MATHS
◗ The skill of manipulating mental images of numbers in your head is invaluable to maths.

WHAT TO LOOK FOR
◗ Can the child talk about the mental images in his head?
◗ Can the child think of three objects and mentally add two more and describe the image in her head?

MORE HELP NEEDED
◗ Have marbles and a 'magic box' available for any children who may want to use them to help them with the activity.
◗ Children who have difficulty need more practice of arranging objects in patterns, and games involving counting spots on dominoes and dice.

---

18 MORE OR LESS?
MATHS FOCUS – NUMBER KIT 1

Name _____

Magic box

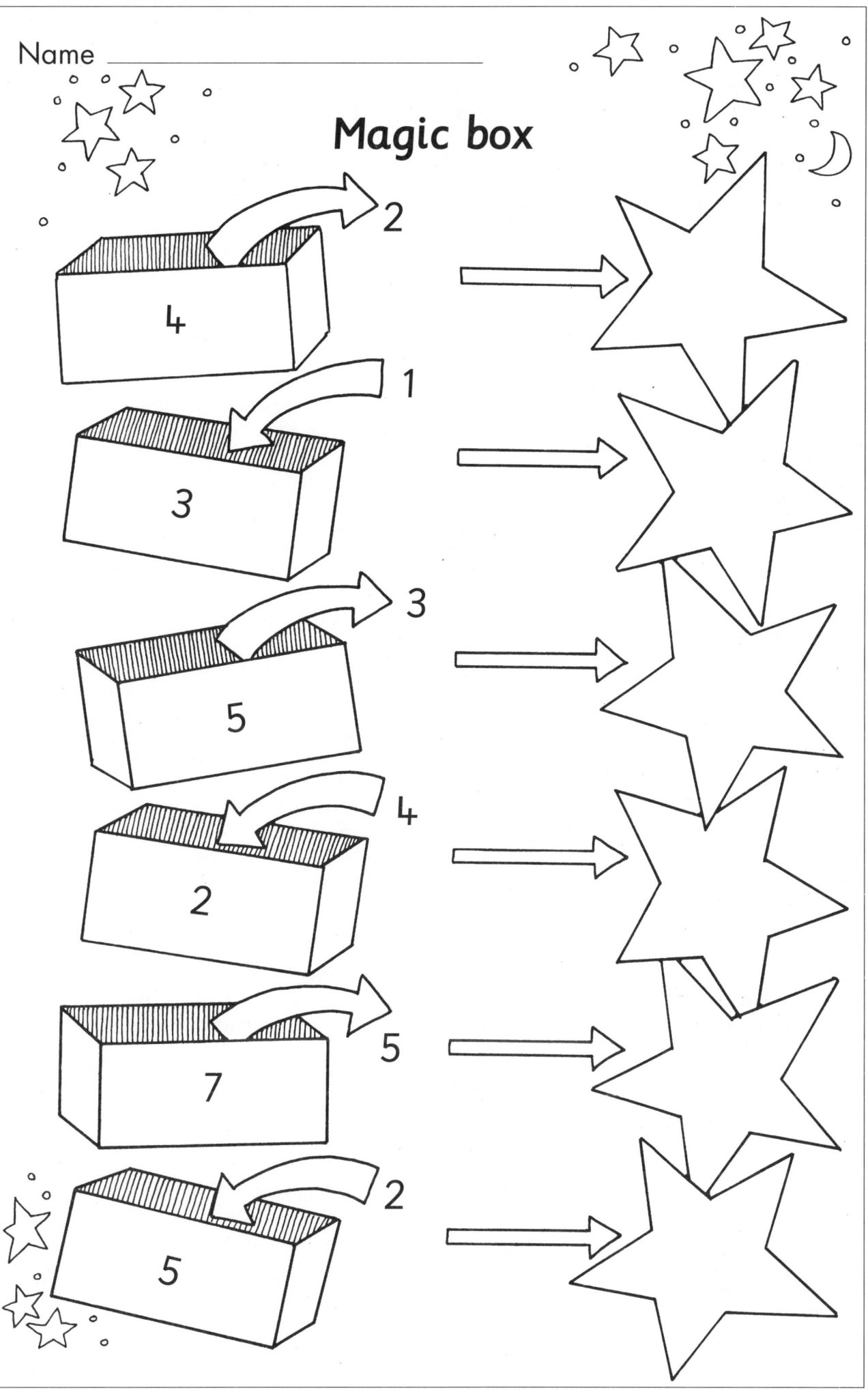

USING & APPLYING

PROBLEM SOLVING
◗ Choose appropriate objects.
◗ Work independently.
◗ Guess, then check.
COMMUNICATION
◗ Record systematically.
◗ Discuss the work.
LOGICAL REASONING
◗ Make reasonable guesses which are getting closer each time.
◗ Understand that the smaller the object the bigger the number.

TALK ABOUT

◗ 'Did you make a good guess?'
◗ 'Are your guesses getting any closer each time?'
◗ 'Which was your closest guess so far?'
◗ 'How do you work out how many you have actually got?'

HERE'S THE MATHS

◗ Looking at arrangements of objects and developing a visual sense of their pattern will help children to develop skills in mentally manipulating numbers.

WHAT TO LOOK FOR

◗ Can the child make sensible guesses?
◗ Can the child explain how he arrived at his guess?

MORE HELP NEEDED

◗ Children who make wild guesses and have difficulty with the counting need activities which help to develop their counting skills and encourage them to look for number patterns in arrangements of objects.

REINFORCEMENT ACTIVITY

Guess how many

Key aims
◗ To encourage a mental vision of addition.
◗ To encourage estimation of answers.

What you need
◗ 1 activity sheet per child
◗ selection of objects such as cubes, bricks, polydrons (not too small) each in a container
◗ pencils

The activity
◗ Explain to the children that they are going to choose an object, and draw one of these on the first pair of hands on their sheet.
◗ Next they pick up two handfuls of the object and guess how many they think they have altogether. Emphasise that you are wanting a good 'guess', and that they are not to count them to give an accurate answer.
◗ Show them where on the sheet to write their guess, and then where to write down the actual number once they have checked it by counting. You may want them to draw in the number of objects in each hand on their sheet before they check the total by counting.
◗ Tell them that they will then pick a different object and do the same again and repeat this to complete the sheet.
◗ Encourage the children to look around the room to see what else they could use for sets of objects.
◗ Leave them to work on their own.

Extension idea
◗ Encourage the children to do the activity again, using smaller objects. This will involve them with the addition of bigger numbers.

---

20 MORE OR LESS?
MATHS FOCUS – NUMBER KIT 1

Name _____

Guess how many

Guess   Check

Continue on the back of this sheet.

PHOTOCOPIABLE

USING & APPLYING

PROBLEM SOLVING
- Work systematically.
- Work independently.
- Select the appropriate mathematics.

COMMUNICATION
- Record appropriately.
- Discuss the work.

LOGICAL REASONING
- Notice and explain the pattern.
- Show an understanding of the subtractions.

TALK ABOUT

- 'How many worms are left now?'
- 'Can you spot a pattern?'
- 'What is 5 take away 1?'
- 'How many worms are inside the fish?'
- 'How many worms are back in the water?'
- 'Can you spot a pattern?'
- 'What is 3 add 1 more?'

HERE'S THE MATHS

- This activity gives children a visual model of the 'taking away' aspect of subtraction, which will help them to 'see' the process in their heads.
- It also shows how addition is linked to subtraction.
- They also become familiar with the pattern of 'one more' and 'one less'.

WHAT TO LOOK FOR

- Can the child do the subtractions?
- Does the child see the pattern?
- Can the child see a link between addition and subtraction?

MORE HELP NEEDED

- Children who work randomly and can't see a pattern in the subtraction, need more practice at looking for number patterns in other activities.

22 MORE OR LESS?
MATHS FOCUS – NUMBER KIT 1

REINFORCEMENT ACTIVITY

Fish and the worms

Key aims
- To give practical experience of adding 1 and taking away 1.
- To build addition and subtraction facts to 5.

What you need
- 1 activity sheet per child
- coloured pens and pencils
- scissors

Organisation
- You may want to stick the activity sheets on to card before giving them to the children. You will need to cut the split by the fish's mouth on each sheet.

The activity
- Give each child a copy of the activity sheet and let them colour in their fish and worms and then cut off the strip of worms, as indicated by the scissor line.

- Show the children how to make their fish eat one worm at a time.
- Talk through the wording on the sheet. You may want to do the first one together, asking the children to all make their fish eat just one worm.
- When the children are happy about what to do leave them to do it again, this time recording on their sheet how many worms are left.
- Before they all explore what happens when the fish spits out the worms, you may want to talk about any patterns they can see in the numbers they have recorded so far.
- Now ask them to make all the worms go into the fish's mouth, so that there are none in the water.
- Tell them that the fish is not hungry and spits one out. Show them where this is recorded on the sheet: '0 spits out 1' (where 0 refers to the number of fish in the water). Ask them how many worms are now in the water. Let them continue like this to complete the sheet.

Extension ideas
- Add more worms on to the strip, and do the activity again.
- Let the children make their own 'eating animal', for example a caterpillar eating leaves or a squirrel eating nuts.

USING & APPLYING

PROBLEM SOLVING
◗ Work systematically.
◗ Work as an individual within their pair.
COMMUNICATION
◗ Talk about the game.
LOGICAL REASONING
◗ Work out which two numbers are needed for a certain space.
◗ Make his or her own number picture.

TALK ABOUT

◗ 'How did you work out the answers?'
◗ 'What did you throw to fill in that space?'
◗ 'What do you need to fill in that space?'
◗ 'Are any of the numbers difficult to get? Why?'

HERE'S THE MATHS

◗ If you use one dice with numbers on and one with dots on you will be letting the children practise counting on from one number to another.
◗ Using two dice with dots on encourages the children to use their knowledge of number pattern arrangements and number bonds to see the total.

WHAT TO LOOK FOR

◗ Does the child use the pattern of the dots to see the number?
◗ Does the child use the pattern of the dots to do the addition and see the total?
◗ Is the child able to count on from a number?

MORE HELP NEEDED

◗ Children who need to count the total number of dots are not necessarily doing addition: they may just be counting. Let them look for patterns in number arrangements and count on from small numbers.

REINFORCEMENT ACTIVITY

Number pictures

Key aims
◗ To give a variety of ways of adding two sets/numbers.
◗ To build a bank of addition facts.

What you need
◗ 1 half of the activity sheet per child
◗ coloured pens
◗ various dice (see 'Organisation')

Organisation
◗ The octopus picture already has the numbers written on. The wall on the Humpty Dumpty picture has some spaces where you can put in numbers appropriate for that child. They can be used with two 1–6 dice (numbers or dots).
◗ Any clear colouring book page could be adapted for this type of game by writing on your own numbers. For example, use two 1–3 dice (1, 2, 3, 1, 2, 3) with numbers which only go up to 6.
◗ If you want the children to focus on practical adding, use dice with dots. If you want to encourage them to add in their heads, use dice with numbers. If you want them to do adding by counting on, use one number dice and one with dots. So, for example, if they throw the following dice, they would say '6, 7, 8':

 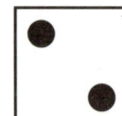

The activity
◗ Give each pair a copy of the same picture each and the appropriate dice.
◗ Explain that they are going to take turns to throw both the dice, add the numbers, then colour the part of their picture which corresponds to the total.
◗ They continue until one of them has coloured the whole of their picture.

Extension ideas
◗ Do the activity again using one 7–12 dice and one 1–6 dice, this time subtracting the smaller number from the larger one, to find which part of the picture to colour. You will need to have numbers from 1–11 on their pictures, such as on the octopus.
◗ Let the children make their own number pictures to play with the game.

Name _____

Number pictures

REINFORCEMENT ACTIVITY

Snake game

Key aims
▶ To practise using a number line, going forwards and backwards.
▶ To develop a knowledge of addition facts.

What you need
▶ 1 half of the activity sheet per child
▶ variety of dice (see 'Organisation')
▶ coloured crayons or pens

Organisation
▶ Give each child either a 0–10 or a 0–20 snake, depending on their ability, and pair them up with a child with the same snake.
▶ Have different dice available such as 1, 2, 3 dice, or 1, 2 dice. You could include ones with spots on and ones with numbers on.

The activity
▶ Ask the children to count along their snake starting at 0. Then going backwards starting at 10 (or 20).
▶ Tell them that they are going to take turns throwing the dice, then moving their counter that many spaces and colouring in where they land on their snake.
▶ Play continues until the first person reaches the end of their snake.
▶ Make sure that the children don't go back to 0 on each throw, and that they don't count the space they are on before moving forward.
▶ Leave them to play the game.

Extension ideas
▶ Give the children the 0–20 snake to play with, if they used the 0–10 one first.
▶ Use a different dice, for example, 2, 0, 2, 0, 2, 0 and explore the pattern of spaces landed on (even numbers only). You could give them number lines on which to record their patterns.
▶ Play the game backwards, starting at 10 (or 20).
▶ Use the larger snake on the postermat (and on page 48) to play the game. This has numbers up to 50.

USING & APPLYING

PROBLEM SOLVING
▶ Work independently within the pair.
▶ Work systematically.
COMMUNICATION
▶ Record appropriately.
▶ Talk about the game.
LOGICAL REASONING
▶ Realise that the higher the number on the dice the further forward they will go, and the smaller the number the less distance they will go.

TALK ABOUT

▶ 'Have you coloured the same spaces as your partner? If not, why not?'
▶ 'Which number moved you on the most?'
▶ 'Which number moved you on the least? Why is that?'
▶ 'Can you think of a different way to play this game?'
▶ 'With the 0–2 dice have you coloured in the same spaces as your partner? Why do you think this has happened?'
(See 'Extension ideas'.)

HERE'S THE MATHS

▶ This activity presents numbers in a line, which is important in building up a mental image of how numbers work.

WHAT TO LOOK FOR

▶ Can the child make proper moves and jumps on the number track, without counting the space she is on?
▶ Does the child realise that the higher the number on the dice the further forward along the snake she will move?

MORE HELP NEEDED

▶ Children who have difficulty making the moves along the track, need more practice playing simple board games.

26 MORE OR LESS?
MATHS FOCUS – NUMBER KIT 1

Name _____

Snake game

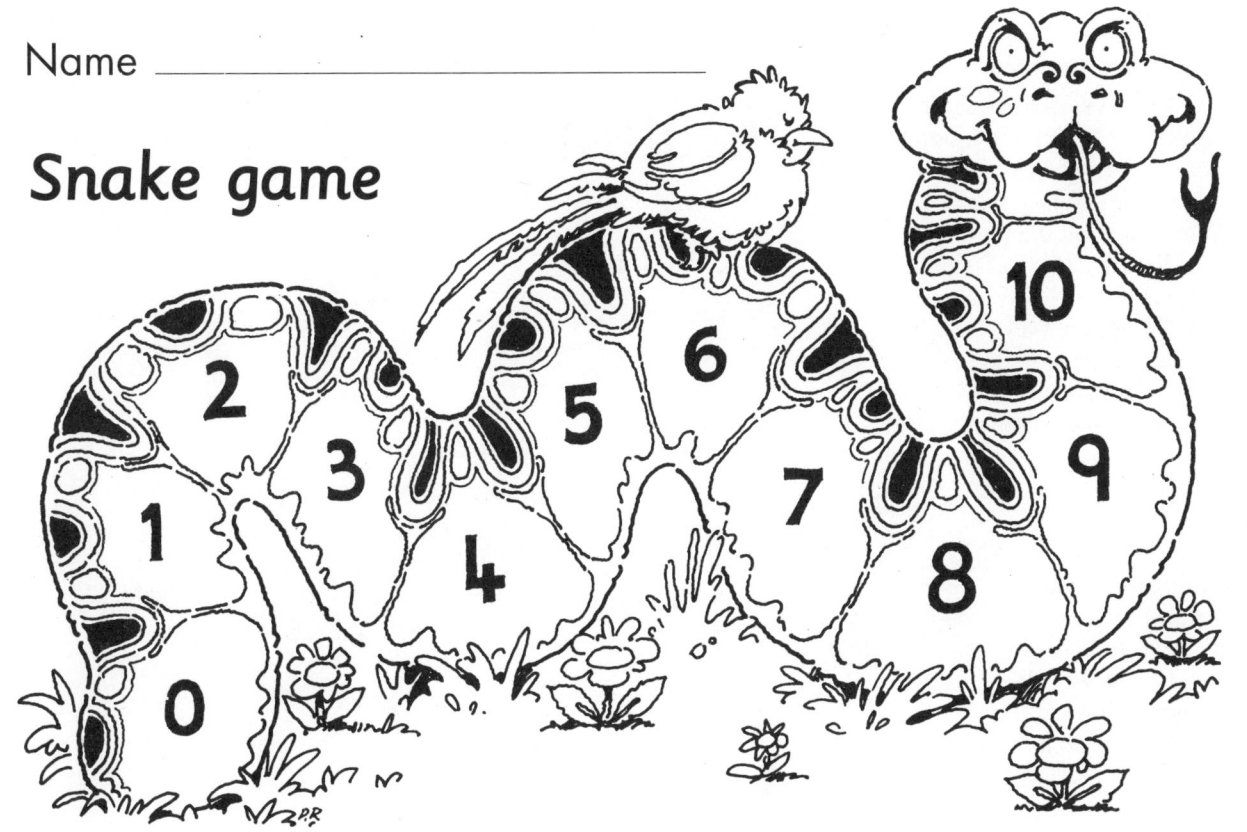

Colour in the numbers you land on.

Name _____

Snake game

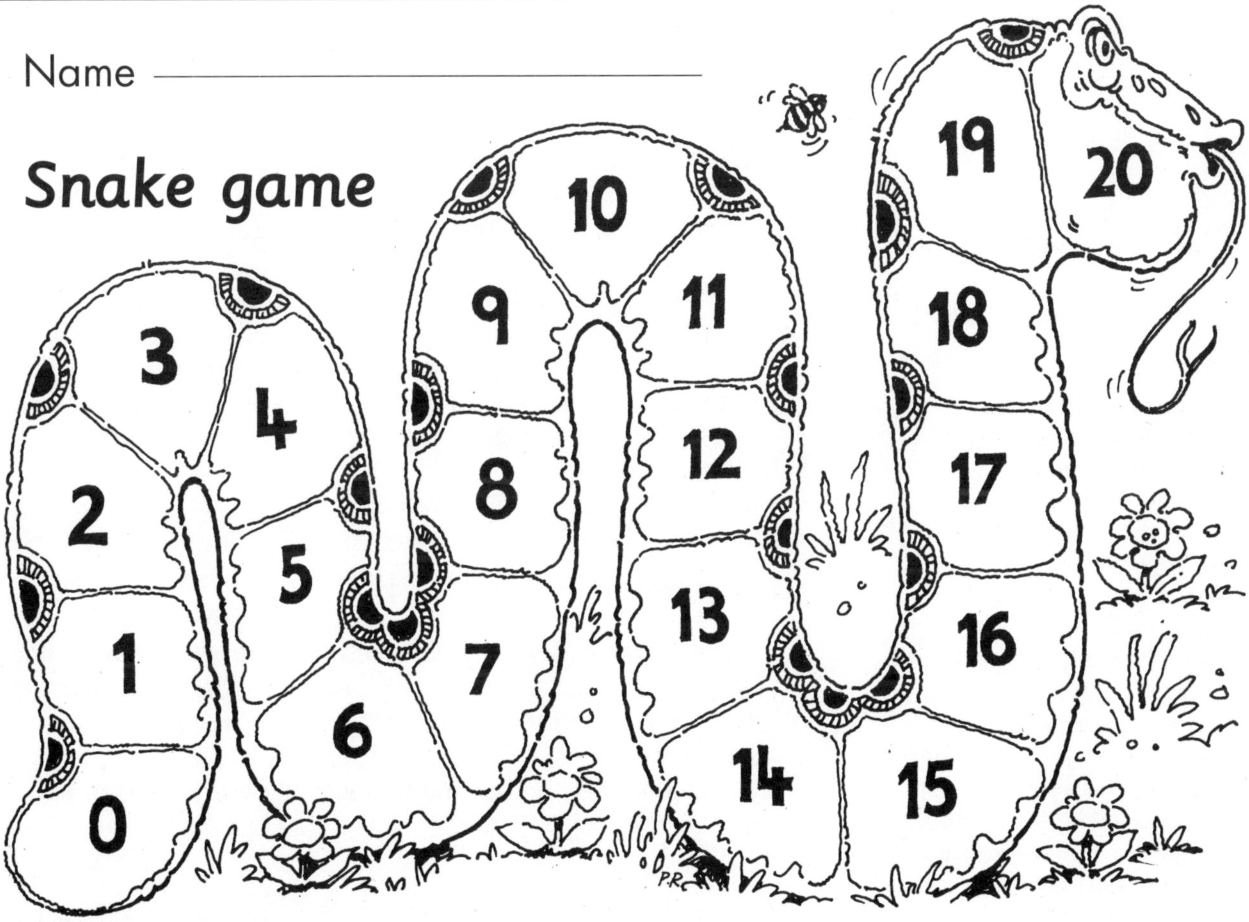

Colour in the numbers you land on.

PHOTOCOPIABLE

MORE OR LESS?
MATHS FOCUS – NUMBER KIT 1

27

USING & APPLYING

PROBLEM SOLVING
- Match each object in the book to the correct number.
- Work methodically.

COMMUNICATION
- Discuss what is involved.

LOGICAL REASONING
- Work out answers to the questions.
- Devise own method of recording.

TALK ABOUT

- 'How are you putting the numbers in order?'
- 'Which number should come next?'
- 'Where do you get to if you move on one square along from the apple?'
- 'Where do you get to if you move back one square from the butterfly?'
- 'Which number is one more/one less than the grasshopper?'
- 'What do you notice about the numbers in the book? What if we read the book backwards?'

HERE'S THE MATHS

- Using a number line to add and subtract provides a useful mental model.

WHAT TO LOOK FOR

- Can the child order the numbers?
- Can the child use the number line to add and subtract 1?

MORE HELP NEEDED

- Children who have difficulty putting the numbers in order need practice ordering numbers and sets of objects.
- Children who have difficulty using the number line for addition and subtraction could use a floor number line to jump forwards and backwards.

28 MORE OR LESS?
MATHS FOCUS – NUMBER KIT 1

REINFORCEMENT ACTIVITY

Counting sheep

Key aims
- To develop the concept of adding 1 and taking away 1.
- To practise using a number line to add 1 and take away 1.

What you need
- popular counting book such as *When Sheep Cannot Sleep* by Satoshi Kitamura (Red Fox)
- 1 activity sheet per child
- coloured pens/crayons
- scissors
- glue
- long strips of card
- paper

Introduction
- Read the story *When Sheep Cannot Sleep* or another popular counting book to the children and talk about what is happening on each page.

The activity
- Ask the children to use the grid on the activity sheet to show what is happening on the first ten pages of the book. Tell them that they only need to draw each object once because the number shows how many there are.
- When they have finished their pictures, tell them to cut out each square and shuffle them up.
- Now ask the children to put their pictures in order and then stick them on to their strip of card.
- The children can then count forwards and backwards along their strip – which is now a number line – and answer specific questions about which object is one on or one back from another object.
- Let them record their findings.

Extension ideas
- Use their number line to record systematically what happens when you move along a specific number of squares each time.
- Do the same for moving back a specific number of squares each time.
- Extend their number line to cover all objects in the book.

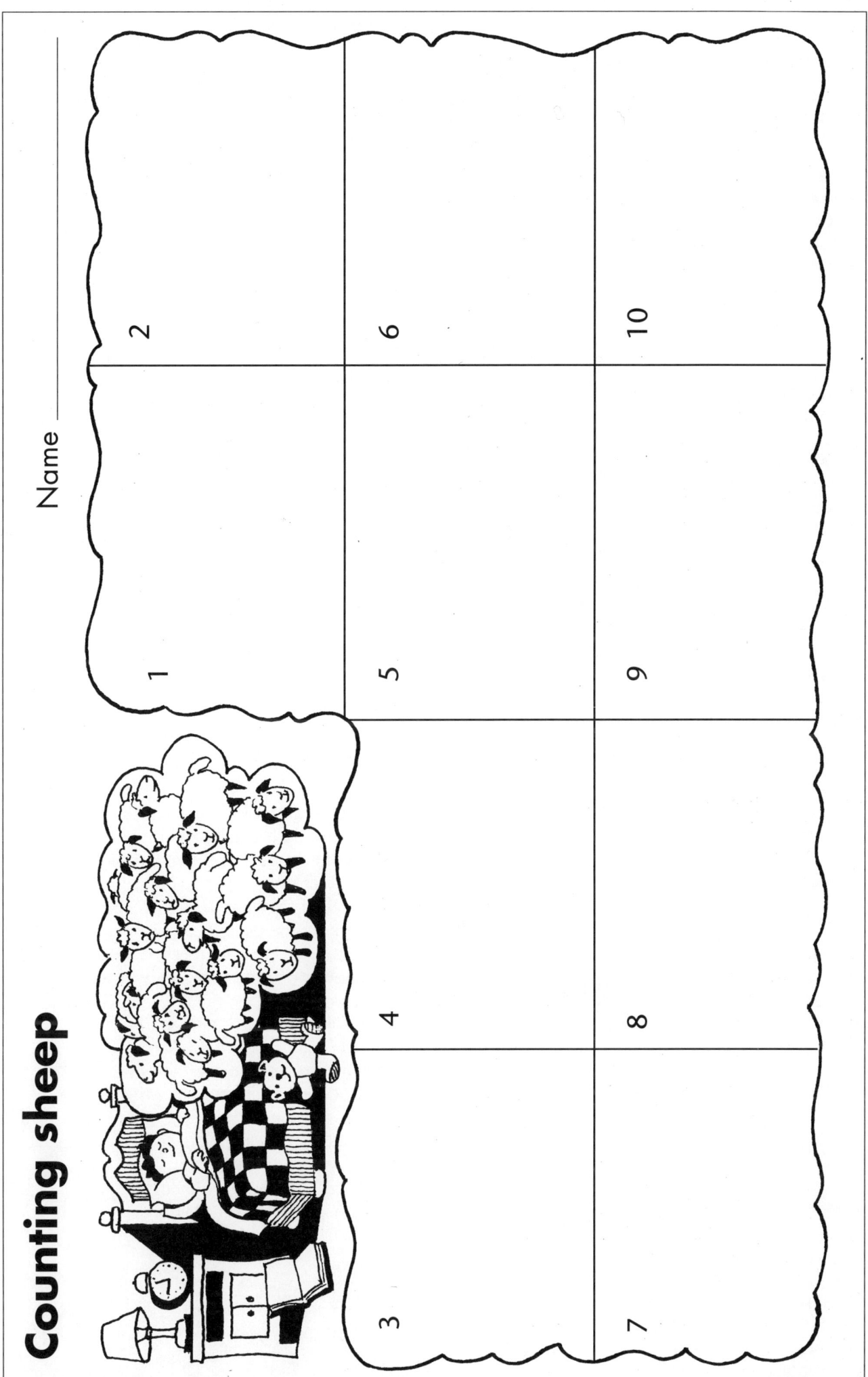

USING & APPLYING

PROBLEM SOLVING
- Work collaboratively.
- Devise own method of recording.

COMMUNICATION
- Discuss work.
- Record appropriately.

LOGICAL REASONING
- Work out the difference.

TALK ABOUT

- 'How many more cubes does your green tower have than your partner's?'
- 'What two numbers are involved here? What's the difference between them?'
- 'Who has the tallest red tower? How many cubes are there?'
- 'Who has the shortest tower of all? How many cubes are there?'
- 'How many more cubes does the tallest tower have than the shortest one?'
- 'How can we record this?'

HERE'S THE MATHS

- In everyday life the difference form of subtraction is more common than take away. Children see each form of subtraction as different, and need to practise each before they realise that they are the same operation.

WHAT TO LOOK FOR

- Can the child compare the towers and say the difference?
- Can the child record independently?

MORE HELP NEEDED

- Some children may need to talk about real situations, such as comparing numbers of children with red/blue sweaters standing in a line, before they can grasp the idea of difference. You may need to introduce language such as: 'more than', 'fewer than', 'the difference between'.

REINFORCEMENT ACTIVITY

Towers

Key aims
- To introduce the concept of 'difference between two numbers', in a practical context.
- To record difference pictorially.

What you need
- at least 1 activity sheet per child
- small coloured interlocking cubes of three different colours, 12 in total per pair
- three colour dice (two faces of each of three colours) – 1 per pair
- coloured pens
- 1 3x4 grid or 1 dozen egg box per pair

Organisation
- Make sure that the colours on the colour dice correspond to the colours of the interlocking cubes.
- You could give each pair four of each coloured cube, or you may want to give them a random amount of each colour to make up the 12.

The activity
- Give each pair 12 cubes and ask them to put one cube on each grid section (or in each egg-box compartment).
- Explain how to play the game. Tell them that they are to take turns to throw their colour dice and collect from the grid one cube of the colour that they throw. If there are no cubes left of the colour shown by the dice, they miss a turn. Play stops when there are no cubes left.
- They then make towers with the cubes they have collected.
- Show them the activity sheet and tell them that they are to record both of their red towers on their sheet and compare them to see the difference in number of cubes. Tell them to write the difference at the top of the two towers. They then do the same for each of their towers in the other two colours.
- Let them do the activity again – give them another activity sheet each for the recording.

Extension idea
- Use the cubes to explore other differences between towers, for example, to find out how many more 4 is than 2.

30 MORE OR LESS?
MATHS FOCUS – NUMBER KIT 1

Name _____

Towers

Draw your towers.

PHOTOCOPIABLE

MORE OR LESS?
MATHS FOCUS – NUMBER KIT 1

31

ENRICHMENT ACTIVITY

Coloured fish

Key aims
- To consolidate knowledge of addition and subtraction facts.
- To consolidate knowledge of number bonds.

What you need
- 1 activity sheet per child
- yellow, red, blue and orange coloured pens

Organisation
- If the children have not experienced a 'key' before you will need to explain how to use it. For example, draw a circle with '4' in, coloured in blue and a circle with '3' in, coloured in red. Ask the children what colour is '4' and what colour is '5'. Ask them to tell you what colour 2 + 2 gives you.

The activity
- Give the children a copy of the activity sheet each and explain the colour chart. Make sure that they can read the words. If they are not confident with this you may want to get them to colour over each word in the relevant colour.
- Explain that they need to work out the 'answer' for each part of the fish and then find the 'special colour' for that piece by looking in the box. You may want to do one of the pieces together to make sure they know what to do.
- Leave them to finish colouring the fish on their own. Encourage them to work out the answers mentally.

Extension ideas
- Let the children make their own 'colour animals' for friends to use to colour in. Encourage them to do them themselves first to check that they have covered each number in their key.
- Play 'Number bingo'. Give the children a 2 x 3 grid and ask them to write in one number from between 0 and 20 into each square. Call out 'sums', such as 3 + 2, 7 – 3 and so on. If the answer is one of their numbers they cover it with a counter. Continue until the first player has a 'full house'.

USING & APPLYING

PROBLEM SOLVING
- Use the key.
- Work systematically.

COMMUNICATION
- Talk about the work.
- Talk about how quickly he or she can work out the answers.

LOGICAL REASONING
- Spot that they can work out some answers at the same time, such as 3 + 1 and 1 + 3.

TALK ABOUT
- 'What colour do you need to use for this bit? Why?'
- 'Can you see any parts which you think will be coloured in the same colour?'
- 'For which parts of the fish did you find it easiest to work out which colour to use?'

HERE'S THE MATHS
- This activity makes addition and subtraction more abstract and assumes that the children have built up mental images of numbers in order to combine them, and can use strategies such as counting on and back.

WHAT TO LOOK FOR
- Can the child use his knowledge of numbers flexibly for addition and subtraction?
- Can the child spot the pairs?
- Can the child predict a piece which will be the same colour?

MORE HELP NEEDED
- Have objects available for children who need them to help with the counting.
- If children find these calculations difficult they need more practice of adding and subtracting using objects and number lines.

Coloured fish

Name _____

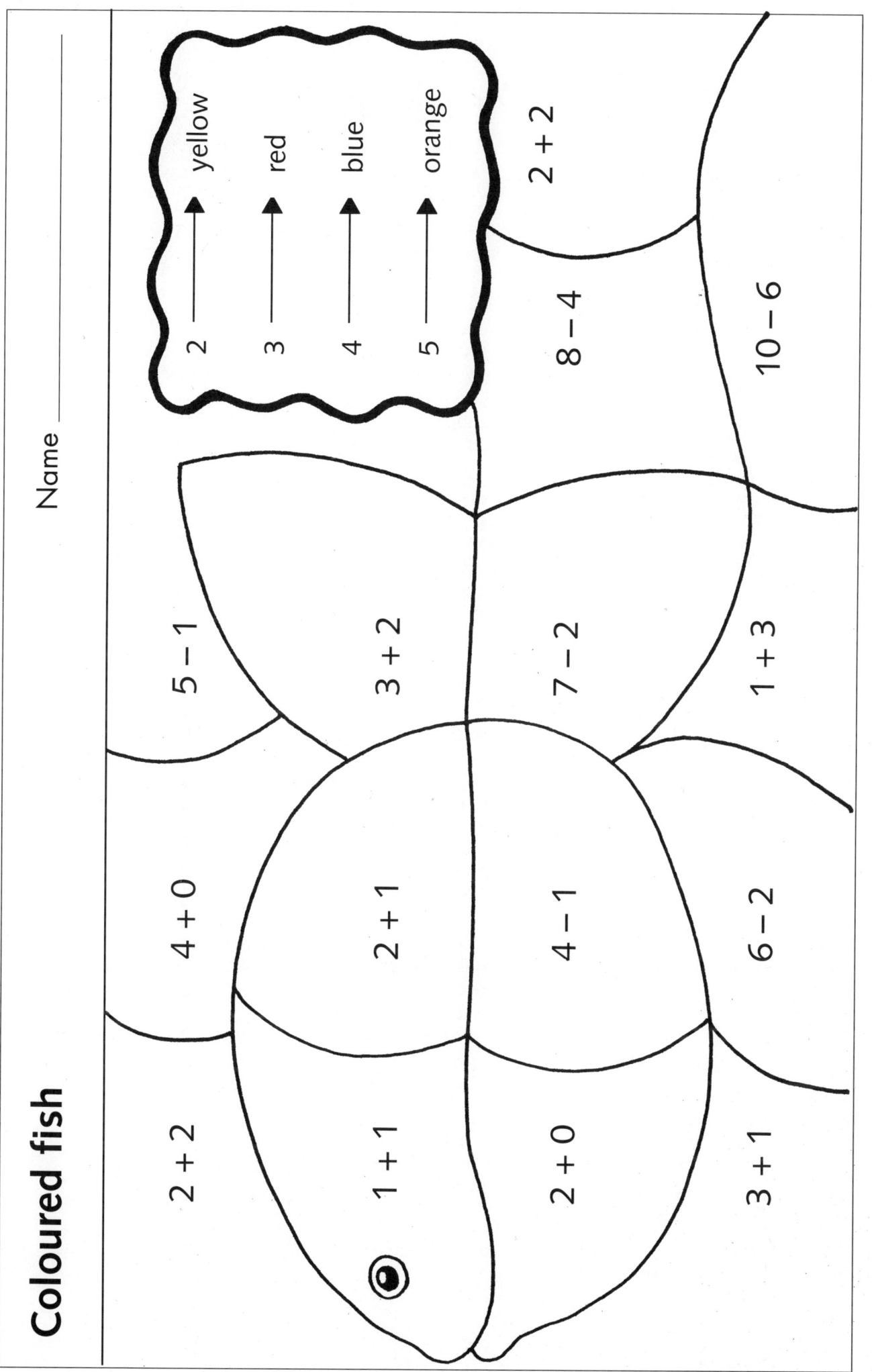

PHOTOCOPIABLE

MORE OR LESS?
MATHS FOCUS – NUMBER KIT 1

ENRICHMENT ACTIVITY

Apple pairs

Key aims
- To encourage quick mental addition.
- To continue to consolidate addition number bonds.

What you need
- 1 set of apple cards per group made from 'Apple pairs' activity sheet (opposite) and 'Apple pairs' resource sheet on page 45 (see 'Organisation')
- scissors
- stop-watch or egg timer

Organisation
- Stick the activity sheet and resource sheet together, back to back, to cut out and make two-sided cards. You could sandwich card between the two sheets and cover each cut-out card with clear self-adhesive plastic to make them more long-lasting.

The activity
- Spread out the cards on the table with the apples face up.
- Ask the children to take turns in turning over two apples.
- If they give the same number then they keep both cards, if not they put them face down on the table again in the same place as before.
- Leave them to continue until all pairs have been collected.
- When they have finished spread out all the cards face up for them to look at. Ask them how many cards they can see which would match one particular number, say 6. Ask them to think of something else to write on a card which would make this number (a different addition, or a subtraction sum).
- Now let the children play the game again, this time timing how quickly they can collect all the cards. You could instead give them an egg timer and challenge them to complete the game before all the sand has run out.

Extension ideas
- Give the children more cards to add to this game, including some subtraction sums.
- Let the children make some more cards which make the numbers 6, 7 and 8.
- Let them make their own pairs game with these cards.

USING & APPLYING
PROBLEM SOLVING
- Use a strategy to work out where the cards are.
- Work collaboratively.

COMMUNICATION
- Explain what she or he is doing and how he or she is working them out.

LOGICAL REASONING
- Notice that some number bonds give the same answer.

TALK ABOUT
- 'Do these two give the same number? How do you know?'
- 'How many cards make this number?'
- 'Did you get any quicker at playing the game?'
- 'How can you check that all the cards have a pair and that there won't be any left over at the end?'

HERE'S THE MATHS
- This activity assumes children have a good understanding of simple addition. It's purpose is to give further practice of mental addition.

WHAT TO LOOK FOR

- Does the child become more fluent with the addition as she does the activity?

MORE HELP NEEDED
- Children who have difficulty with this activity should not continue with it. Give them more practice of addition using objects and number lines, and talking about the patterns of numbers.

Apple pairs

6	7	8
4 + 2	5 + 2	5 + 3
6	7	8
3 + 3	4 + 3	4 + 4

PHOTOCOPIABLE

USING & APPLYING

PROBLEM SOLVING
- Devise a way for solving the problem.
- Work systematically.
- Work independently.

COMMUNICATION
- Record appropriately.
- Discuss the work.

LOGICAL REASONING
- 'Count on' when adding.
- Find that for some shapes the same number can be used in each corner to make the middle one.

TALK ABOUT

- 'How are you working it out?'
- 'What is the biggest number you can make?'
- 'Have you found all possibilities for making this number for this shape? How do you know?'

HERE'S THE MATHS

- Children are required to use their knowledge of numbers flexibly and to work mentally using a combination of addition and subtraction.

WHAT TO LOOK FOR

- Does the child use a variety of numbers, to come up with a range of combinations?
- Does the child talk about her results, showing an understanding of the patterns of how numbers are made up?

MORE HELP NEEDED

- Make available number lines, counters and calculators for those who want to use them.
- Let children who are having difficulty, or are using a limited range of numbers, use objects to show the quantities involved.

ENRICHMENT ACTIVITY

Number shapes

Key aims
- To extend understanding and use of addition.
- To encourage mental addition.
- To encourage 'counting on' when adding.

What you need
- 1 activity sheet per child
- pencils and paper

Organisation
- Fill in different numbers inside the shapes on each child's activity sheet, so that they can work individually.
- You may want to leave some of the shapes without numbers in so that the children can invent their own.

The activity
- Explain to the children that you want the numbers they put on the corners of the shape to add up to the number in the middle of that shape.

For example:

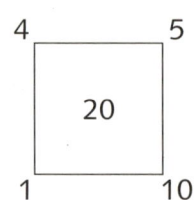 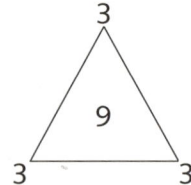

- Show them some examples, until you are sure they are confident about what to do.
- Leave them to complete their own sheet.

Extension ideas
- Investigate how many different ways there are to make a square whose corners add up to 10.
- Investigate whether there any 'number shapes' where you have the same number in each corner. You may want first to give them one particular example to investigate, such as 20 for a square, and let them try different possibilities until they see that the number 5 can be used in each corner.

MORE OR LESS?
MATHS FOCUS – NUMBER KIT 1

Name _____

Number shapes

Do some more on the back of this sheet.

PHOTOCOPIABLE

MORE OR LESS?
MATHS FOCUS – NUMBER KIT 1

USING & APPLYING

PROBLEM SOLVING
◗ Work systematically.
◗ Work collaboratively and individually.
COMMUNICATION
◗ Explain work and recording.
LOGICAL REASONING
◗ Work out the difference.
◗ Show an ability to check answers – maybe with cubes.

TALK ABOUT

◗ 'If you start from the 6, how many jumps to get to the 9?'
◗ 'What is the difference between these two numbers?'
◗ 'How are you working out the difference?'
◗ 'Can you check your answers using the cubes?'

HERE'S THE MATHS

◗ This activity involves a more complex use of the number line to count on and back from one number to another, in order to compare those numbers. This skill is important to developing flexible mental maths strategies.

WHAT TO LOOK FOR

◗ Can the child identify a number on the line and count the jumps to another point on the line?
◗ Can the child compare two numbers on the line by jumping forwards or back between them, and say, for example, that 6 is 2 more than 4, and that the difference between 6 and 4 is 2?

MORE HELP NEEDED

◗ Children who can use a number line for simple jumping on and back, but cannnot use it for finding the difference need more practice – a floor number line helps, making physical jumps back and forth.

ENRICHMENT ACTIVITY

What's the difference?

Key aims
◗ To develop an understanding of difference.
◗ To use a number line to work out the difference between two numbers.

What you need
◗ 1 activity sheet per child
◗ 0–20 number cards, 1 set per pair (see resource sheets on pages 46–47)
◗ pencils
◗ cubes

Organisation
◗ Cut out the numbers from the resource sheets beforehand – you may wish to put them on card and cover them with clear self-adhesive plastic.
◗ Have cubes to hand for any children who need them.

The activity
◗ Put the number cards in a pile face down. Tell the children that in their pairs they are going to turn over one card each then work out the difference between them (using cubes if they wish).
◗ When they have had plenty of practice, give out the activity sheets.
◗ Explain that they are going to work out the differences on the sheet using the 0–10 number line given.
◗ Have a few goes with the children. Ensure that they do not count the number they start on, but count the actual jumps. Make sure that they understand that the difference, for example, between 9 and 6 is 3.
◗ Leave them to complete the sheet.

Extension ideas
◗ Use cubes to explore various pairs of numbers which all have the same difference, for example 5.
◗ Use the cards to write number statements. Give them the +, – and = sign cards if they want to use them.
◗ Use a 0–20 number line to set number jump tasks for their partner, in the style of those on the activity sheet. They can then complete their partner's sheet.
◗ Use the postermat for a game which involves throwing two 1–6 dice (or 1–3 depending on what level you want to cover) and working out the difference to make their move. They could use the number line to help them calculate how many spaces to jump.

MORE OR LESS?
MATHS FOCUS – NUMBER KIT 1

What's the difference?

Name _____

0 1 2 3 4 5 6 7 8 9 10

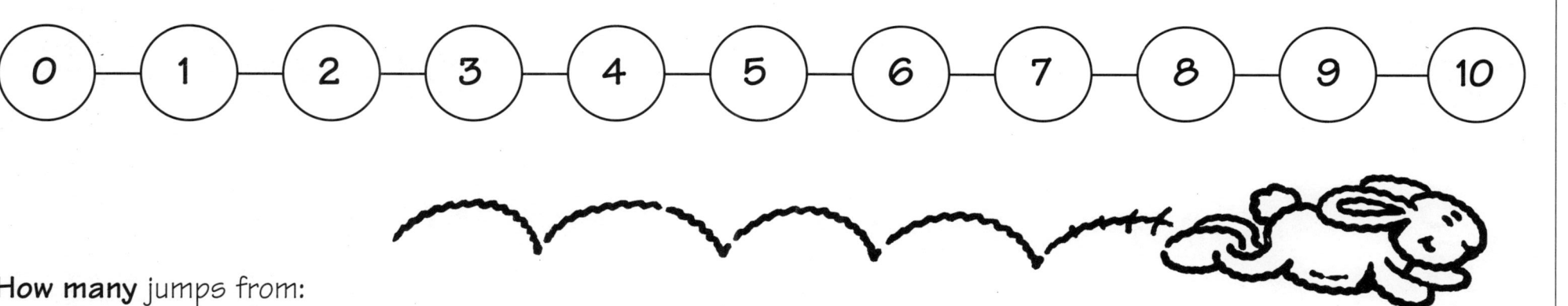

How many jumps from:

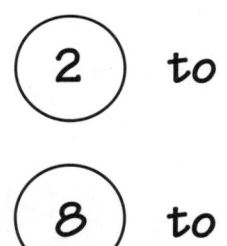

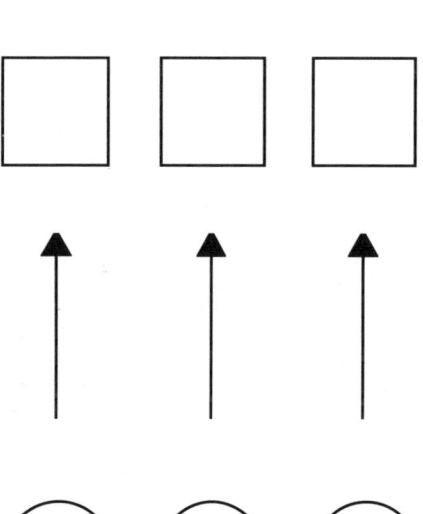

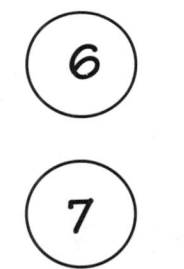

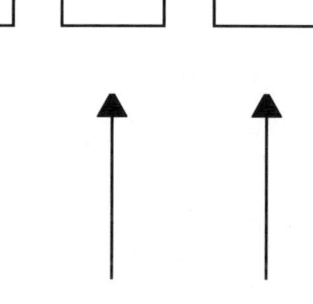

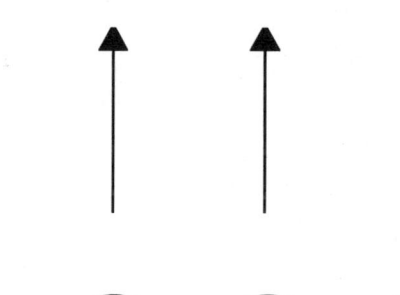

1 to 3 □
4 to 5 □
2 to 6 □
8 to 7 □

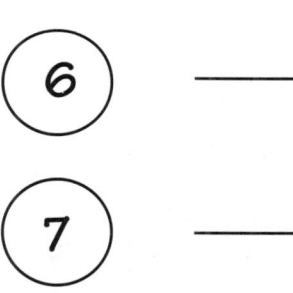

4 to 7 □
9 to 5 □
5 to 10 □
10 to 4 □

PHOTOCOPIABLE

MORE OR LESS?
MATHS FOCUS – NUMBER KIT 1
39

ENRICHMENT ACTIVITY

Calculator adding

Key aims
- To become familiar with the calculator constant function.
- To explore the number patterns created.
- **Also covered**: consolidating existing knowledge of addition facts; experiencing repeated addition.

What you need
- 1 calculator per child
- 1 activity sheet per child
- pencils

Organisation
- Ensure the children are familiar with using a calculator, and show an understanding of calculator digits. Practise making the digit shapes with used matchsticks.
- Make sure you know how the constant function on your classroom calculators works. On some calculators you press:

| number | + | = | and then keep pressing | = |

| number | + | + | = | and then keep pressing | = |

- You may need to amend the activity sheet to match your classroom calculators, by deleting a [+] sign.

The activity
- Give each child a calculator and show them how to 'make the calculator add', by using the constant function.
- Give out the activity sheets and give each child a different number to start with: 1, 2, 3, 4, or 5.
- Tell them to write their number in the flower on the activity sheet and then key in the buttons on their calculator.
- Before they press '=' again explain that they are to 'guess' which number they think the calculator will show and write it down on their activity sheet. They then press the '=' key to check and write the number in the 'check' circle on their sheet.

Extension ideas
- Do the activity again using a different starting number.
- Do the activity without the calculator, using a number line if they want to. They can check their work using the calculator.
- Devise ways to record the patterns discovered. Use the postermat to record the numbers in each pattern.

USING & APPLYING

PROBLEM SOLVING
- Use the constant function in order to solve the problem.
- Work systematically.

COMMUNICATION
- Explain work.
- Record findings.

LOGICAL REASONING
- Make good guesses.
- Make understandable errors (if any).

TALK ABOUT
- 'Were you surprised by any answers?'
- 'Can you see a pattern?'
- 'Why do you think a pattern has happened?'

HERE'S THE MATHS
- Calculators offer a useful way of extending number skills. Children can use them to work back from an answer; to work out the process that has gone on to reach the answer. They also allow you to generate lots of answers quickly, which is useful when exploring a pattern. This activity involves children in looking for the pattern.

WHAT TO LOOK FOR
- Can the child make sensible predictions?
- Does the child understand the difference between predicting and then checking on their calculator?
- Does the child understand what the calculator is doing?

MORE HELP NEEDED
- Children who have difficulty using the calculator need more free activity work exploring what calculators can do, and activities involving simple key-pressing tasks.

40 MORE OR LESS?
MATHS FOCUS – NUMBER KIT 1

Name _____

Calculator adding

Press:

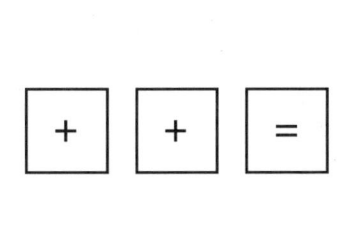

☐+ ☐+ ☐=

| Guess | Check | | Guess | Check |

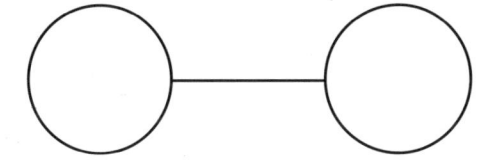

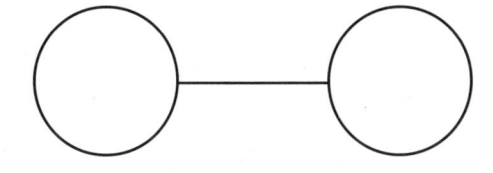

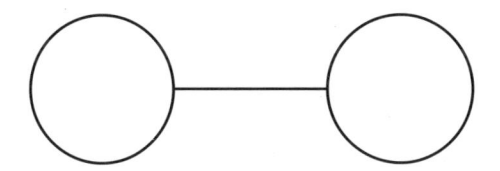

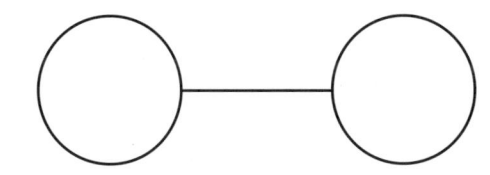

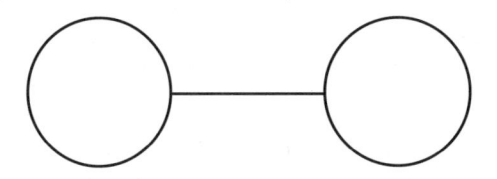

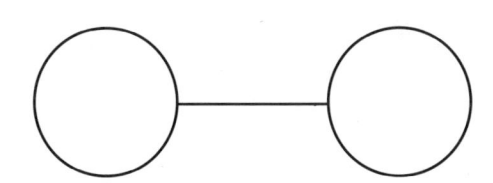

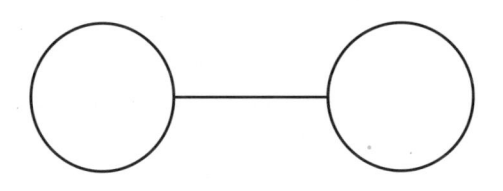

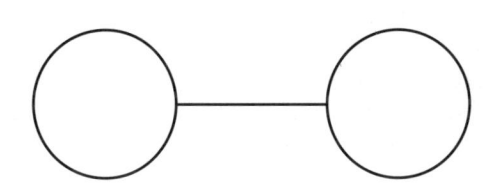

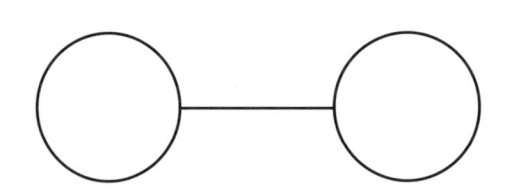

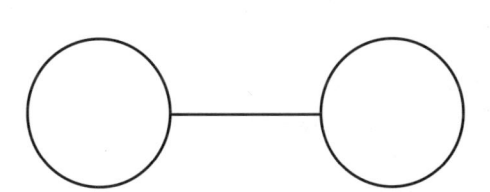

Carry on with this number on the back of this sheet.

PHOTOCOPIABLE

ENRICHMENT ACTIVITY

Secret numbers

Key aims
- To select the mathematics required.
- To consolidate the relationship between addition and subtraction.
- To use a calculator for addition and subtraction.

What you need
- 1 copy of the snake game postermat per pair (or photocopiable version on page 48)
- 1–6 dice per pair or 1–10 spinner
- 1 calculator per child
- 1 counter per child
- small paper pieces
- 1 activity sheet per child
- scissors, sticky tape, pencils

Organisation
- Give each pair a postermat (or copy of page 48) and a dice and each child a counter, piece of paper, pencil and calculator.

The activity
- Ask the children each to put their counter on 25 on the snake and make their calculator show 25.
- Tell them to pick a 'secret number' which is on the snake, but is not 25, and write it down on their piece of paper and then keep it hidden.
- Explain that to play the game they are to take it in turns to throw the dice. They must then choose whether to add or subtract the number they throw to the number on the calculator, to get closer to their 'secret number'. They then move their counter to the number shown on their calculator.
- Continue until the calculator shows their 'secret number'. They then reveal their piece of paper for their partner to check.
- Help the children to make a 0–50 number line from the activity sheet and use this to record what they do.

Extension ideas
- Play the game again but this time choosing two secret numbers and putting two counters each on the 25 space on the snake before they start. They must now choose which counter to move each time.
- Choose a number which is either less than 10 or more than 40 and play the game again.
- Write out their moves. Swap with someone else and let them try to work out what each other's secrets number were.

USING & APPLYING
PROBLEM SOLVING
- Work independently.

COMMUNICATION
- Talk about the difference between addition and subtraction.

LOGICAL REASONING
- Work out that adding a number – you move forwards; and subtracting – you move backwards.

TALK ABOUT
- 'What happens if you add/take away this number?'
- 'Which number was easiest to reach? Why?'
- 'How many goes did it take each of you to reach your number?'

HERE'S THE MATHS
- The children need to do mental calculations to decide whether to tell the calculator to add or subtract the number thrown.

WHAT TO LOOK FOR
- Does the child use addition and subtraction correctly to reach their target?
- Does the child use the calculator with confidence?

MORE HELP NEEDED
- Children who lack confidence using the calculator need to do simpler activities.
- Children unsure of the effect of addition and subtraction need to investigate with the calculator, exploring and describing what happens.

---

42 MORE OR LESS?
MATHS FOCUS – NUMBER KIT 1

Name _____

Secret numbers

Make a 0–50 number line. Use it to record your moves.

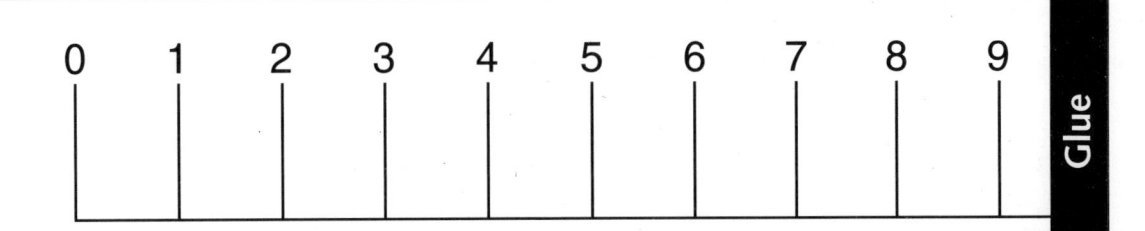

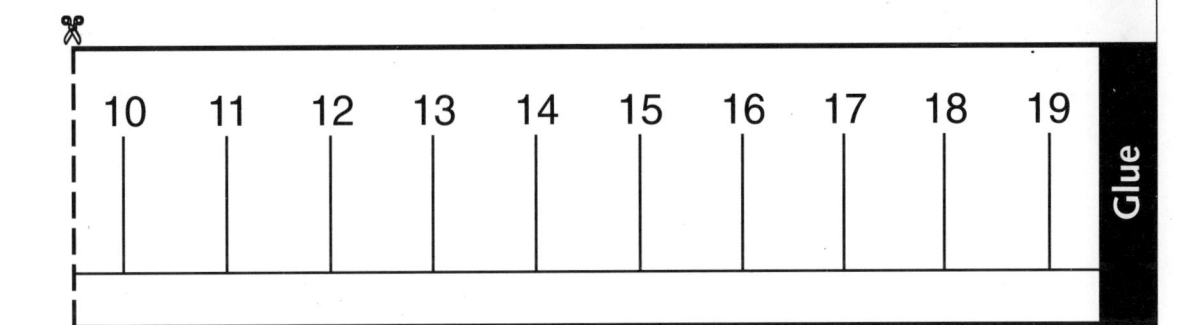

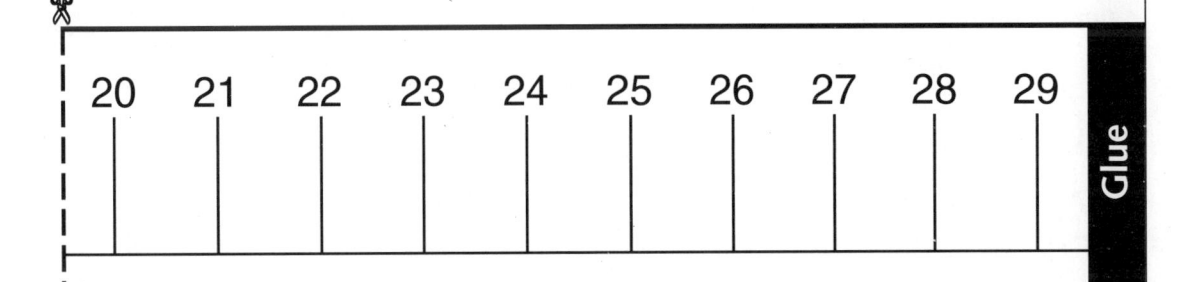

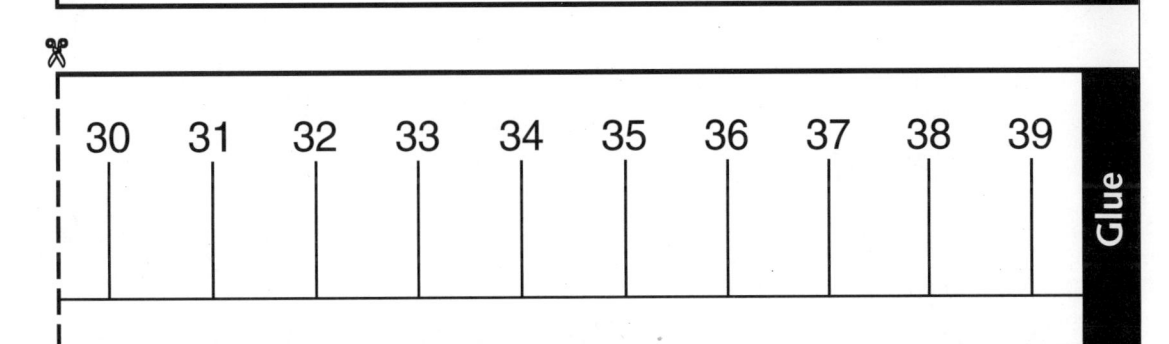

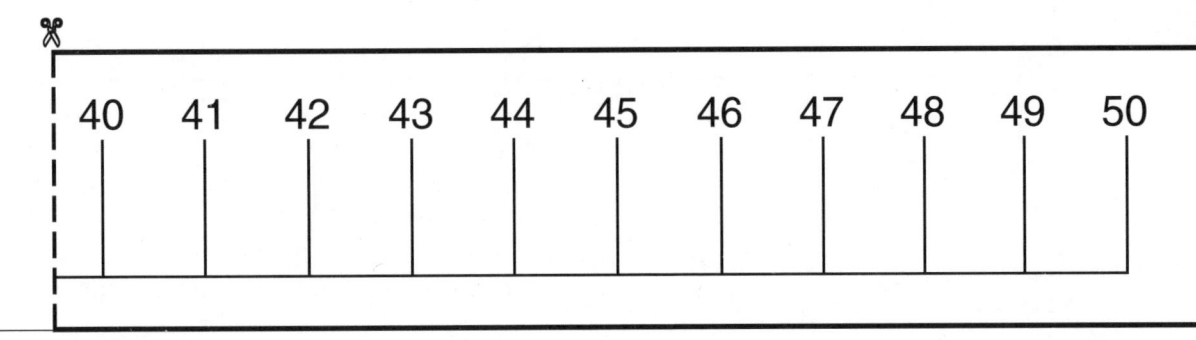

| 0 | 1 | 2 | 3 | 4 | 5 | 6 | 7 | 8 | 9 | Glue |

| 10 | 11 | 12 | 13 | 14 | 15 | 16 | 17 | 18 | 19 | Glue |

| 20 | 21 | 22 | 23 | 24 | 25 | 26 | 27 | 28 | 29 | Glue |

| 30 | 31 | 32 | 33 | 34 | 35 | 36 | 37 | 38 | 39 | Glue |

| 40 | 41 | 42 | 43 | 44 | 45 | 46 | 47 | 48 | 49 | 50 |

PHOTOCOPIABLE

MORE OR LESS?
MATHS FOCUS – NUMBER KIT 1

Name _____

Picking apples

MORE OR LESS?
MATHS FOCUS – NUMBER KIT 1

PHOTOCOPIABLE

Apple pairs

PHOTOCOPIABLE

MORE OR LESS?
MATHS FOCUS – NUMBER KIT 1

0	1	2
3	4	5
6	7	8
9	10	11

MORE OR LESS?
MATHS FOCUS – NUMBER KIT 1

PHOTOCOPIABLE

12	13	14
15	16	17
18	19	20
+	−	=

48 MORE OR LESS?
MATHS FOCUS – NUMBER KIT 1

PHOTOCOPIABLE